The United States

Maine

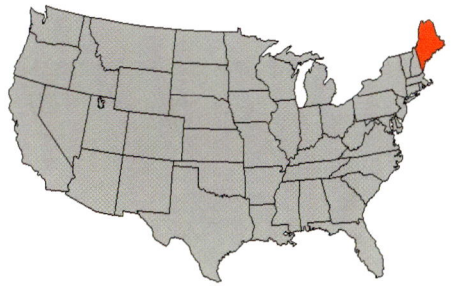

Paul Joseph
ABDO & Daughters

visit us at
www.abdopub.com

Published by Abdo & Daughters, 4940 Viking Drive, Suite 622, Edina, Minnesota 55435. Copyright © 1998 by Abdo Consulting Group, Inc., Pentagon Tower, P.O. Box 36036, Minneapolis, Minnesota 55435 USA. International copyrights reserved in all countries. No part of this book may be reproduced in any form without written permission from the publisher.

Printed in the United States.

Cover and Interior Photo credits: Peter Arnold, Inc., Super Stock

Edited by Lori Kinstad Pupeza
Contributing editor Brooke Henderson
Special thanks to our Checkerboard Kids—Raymond Sherman, Gracie Hansen, Matthew Nichols

All statistics taken from the 1990 census; The Rand McNally Discovery Atlas of The United States. Other sources: Compton's Encyclopedia, 1997; *Maine*, Heinrichs, Children's Press, Chicago, 1989.

Library of Congress Cataloging-in-Publication Data

Joseph, Paul, 1970-
    Maine / Paul Joseph.
    p. cm. -- (The United States)
    Includex Index.
    Summary: Surveys the people, geography, and history of the Pine Tree State.
    ISBN 1-56239-861-X
    1. Maine--Juvenile literature. [1. Maine.] I. Title. II. Series: United States (Series)
    F19.3.J67   1998
    974.1--dc21   97-10498
                                                                                   CIP
                                                                                   AC

Contents

Welcome to Maine 4
Fast Facts About Maine 6
Nature's Treasures 8
Beginnings 10
Happenings 12
Maine's People 18
Splendid Cities 20
Maine's Land 22
Maine at Play 24
Maine at Work 26
Fun Facts 28
Glossary 30
Internet Sites 31
Index 32

Welcome to Maine

Maine is known as the Pine Tree State because most of the state is covered with **forests**. The white pine is the most common tree in the forests of Maine.

The Pine Tree State is the most northeastern state in the country. Besides forests, Maine is dotted with lakes and rivers. The **Atlantic Ocean** washes the state's rocky southern shoreline.

The state probably got its name from the word "main." This word was used in early times to tell the difference between mainland and islands.

Not many people live in Maine. The biggest city has less than 65,000 people. Many people, however, visit this wonderful state.

The forests are filled with many moose, deer, and bears. Maine has the beautiful Acadia National Park. People hunt, fish, boat, ski, and do other outdoor activities in this recreational state.

This small, thinly populated, mostly wilderness state is one of the most important in the country. Not only today, but also long ago.

A lighthouse near Lubec, Maine.

Fast Facts

MAINE
Capital
Augusta (21,325 people)
Area
30,995 square miles
(80,277 sq km)
Population
1,233,223 people
Rank: 38th
Statehood
March 15, 1820
(23rd state admitted)
Principal river
Penobscot River
Highest point
Mount Katahdin; 5,268 feet
(1,606 m)
Largest city
Portland (64,358 people)
Motto
Dirigo
(I direct)
Song
"State of Maine Song"
Famous People
Hannibal Hamlin, Henry Wadsworth Longfellow, Sir Hiram Maxim, Edna St. Vincent Millay

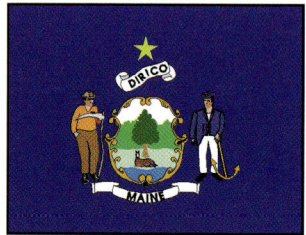

*S*tate Flag

*W*hite Pine Cone and Tassel

*C*hickadee

*E*astern white pine

About Maine
The Pine Tree State

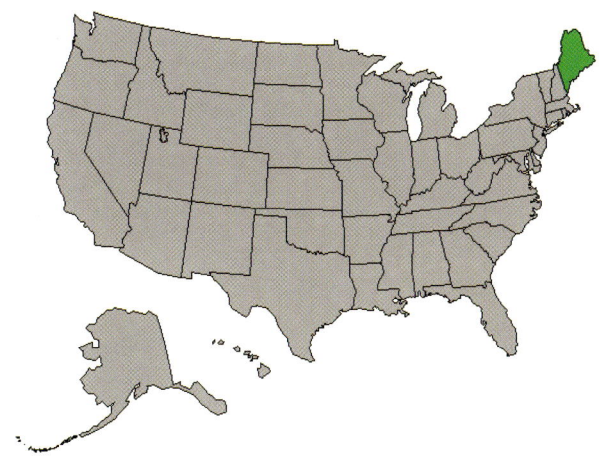

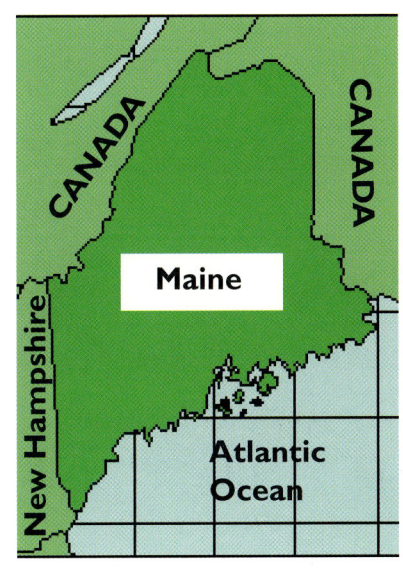

Detail area

Maine's abbreviation

Borders: west (Canada, New Hampshire), north (Canada), east (Canada), south (Atlantic Ocean)

Nature's Treasures

The Pine Forest State's greatest treasure is its valuable timber. **Forests** cover 89 percent of the state. These forests grow mainly pine, spruce, and northern hardwood trees.

Other **natural resources** include **fisheries**, **minerals**, and **farming**. The Fisheries in Maine are among the biggest in the United States. Maine fisheries get the most money from lobster.

The most valuable minerals in Maine are sand, gravel, clay, crushed stone, and limestone.

The soil in Maine is too thin and rocky for a lot of farming. The state has only about 7,000 farms. Maine, however, ranks third in the nation in growing potatoes. Other major **crops** include hay, oats, and corn.

More valuable than Maine's **crops** are poultry, dairy products, and livestock. Apples and wild blueberries are the chief fruits that are grown.

Fishing equipment for catching lobster.

Beginnings

Many thousands of years ago, the area where Maine is now, was covered by glaciers, ice, and snow.

The first known people to live in this region were the Abnakis. Others were the Penobscot and the Passamaquoddy. A series of six wars from 1675 to 1760 took away the power of the **Native Americans** in this area.

Many of the early non-Native American settlers were French people who came from Canada. Another large group of English, Scottish, and Irish also settled in Maine.

England sent **explorers** John and Sebastian Cabot to the coast of Maine. They explored this state in 1508. Because of this, England claimed Maine.

The area of Maine grew slowly. In the early 1800s, however, a boom in building and trading with other countries led to a rapid increase in people.

In 1820, Maine became part of the United States as the 23rd state. Portland was chosen as the capital. In 1832, the capital moved to Augusta.

*Explorer,
Sebastian Cabot.*

Happenings • Happenings • Happenings • Happenings • Happenings • Happeni

Before 1600

The First People of Maine

During the Ice Age, some 20,000 years ago, Maine was covered by snow, ice, and glaciers.

The first known people to live in the area of Maine were the Abnaki nation.

1497-1508: John and Sebastian Cabot sailed along the coast of Maine.

1524: Giovanni da Verrazzano reaches Maine.

Happenings • Happenings • Happenings • Happenings • Happenings • Happenings

Maine
Before 1600

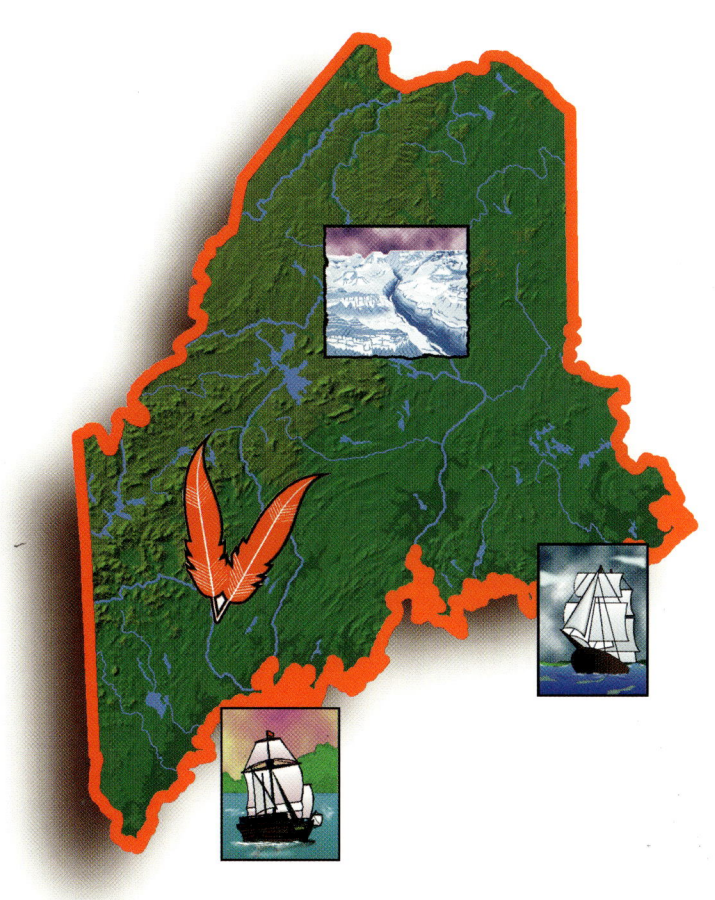

Happenings • Happenings • Happenings • Happenings • Happenings • Happeni

1600s and 1700s

Settlements, Cities, and Wars

1603: Maine became a part of the French province Acadia.

1606: Maine is owned by England.

1641: Gorgeanna, Maine, is America's first chartered city.

1675: The first of six wars in Maine between the **Native Americans** and settlers begin.

1759: The settlers and the Native Americans are more peaceful towards each other.

Happenings • Happenings • Happenings • Happenings • Happenings • Happenings

Maine
1600s and 1700s

Happenings • Happenings • Happenings • Happenings • Happenings • Happeni

1820 to Now

Statehood and Beyond

 1820: Maine becomes the 23rd state on March 15. Portland is the capital.

 1832: The capital is moved to Augusta.

 1965: Gold deposits are found near Pembroke.

 1988: George Bush is elected president of the United States and continues to make Kennebunkport his vacation home.

Happenings • Happenings • Happenings • Happenings • Happenings

Maine
1820 to Now

Maine's People

There are only 1.2 million people that live in Maine today. Only 12 states have less people in them. The first known people to live in Maine were the Abnakis. Many of the first non-native settlers were the French from Canada.

Today, most people living in Maine are white. The state has about 6,000 **Native Americans** and more than 5,000 African Americans.

Many notable people have made the Pine Tree State home. Milton Bradley was born in Vienna, Maine. He thought of the idea of printing board games. The Milton Bradley Company, which he formed in the 1860s, makes many board games that people still play today.

Three of the nation's most famous poets were born in Maine. Henry Wadsworth Longfellow was born in

Portland. Edna St. Vincent Millay was born in Rockland. And Edwin Arlington Robinson was born in Head Tide.

Margaret Chase Smith was a senator in Maine from 1948 to 1973. She almost ran for president in 1964.

As a child, former president George Bush spent many summers in Maine. His great grandfather had bought a **peninsula** in 1899 in Kennebunkport, Maine. When George Bush was elected president of the United States in 1988, he continued to make the beautiful Kennebunkport his vacation home.

Henry Wadsworth Longfellow

Edna St. Vincent Millay

Senator Margaret Chase Smith

Splendid Cities

Maine is one of the only states that doesn't have a single large city. It does, however, have some splendid cities. Maine's largest city and the chief railroad center is Portland. Portland has just under 65,000 people.

Portland is located on a **peninsula** in Casco Bay. It has one of the finest harbors on the Atlantic coast. It also has many small **industries**. Some include fishing, shipbuilding, and paper.

The biggest industrial area of the state is on the Androscoggin River. Lewiston, the state's second largest city, and Auburn, the fourth largest, **manufacture** clothing and shoes.

Augusta, the capital of Maine, is a beautiful river town. Located on the

Kennebec River, Augusta is a great vacation place. It also has Fort Western Museum and the University of Maine.

Kennebunkport was made famous when 41st President George Bush and his family made it their vacation home. To the rest of the people of Maine it has always been a beautiful resort town. Located on the **Atlantic Ocean**, Kennebunkport is great for fishing, boating, or just relaxing.

Corea Harbor, Maine.

Maine's Land

Maine's area is 30,995 square miles (80,277 sq km) including 2,295 square miles (5,944 sq km) of water surface. The Pine Tree State is divided into three distinct areas.

The White Mountains Region goes from New Hampshire to Maine. Most of this land is rugged areas of hills and lakes. In this area is a mountain range called the Longfellow Mountains. Mount Katahdin, the highest point in Maine, is also here. Of the state's 2,500 lakes and ponds, the largest is Moosehead Lake, found in this region.

The New England Upland is a rocky plateau that crosses the entire state from southwest to northeast. It also occupies the entire north. Some sections of this land are rugged and hilly. Most of the land, however, is good for **pastures** and for raising **crops**.

The Seaboard Lowland is a region that follows the Atlantic coast. In this area are the mouths of Maine's largest rivers. The Penobscot, Kennebec, Androscoggin, and Saco each spill into the **Atlantic Ocean**. The beautiful Acadia National Park is in this region.

Acadia National Park, Maine

Maine at Play

Thousands of people visit Maine each year. People visit because there is so much to do. Many of the visitors come from Canada.

In the summer months people hike, bike, run, and walk in the beautiful parks. On the Atlantic coast, people in Maine have fun swimming, sunbathing, fishing, and boating. For more excitement in the water, people ski, sailboard, and jet-ski.

People also visit Maine in the winter. There is downhill skiing, cross-country skiing, and hiking around the mountains. There are also 2,500 lakes and ponds that people enjoy all year long.

Besides visitors and the people of Maine, many presidents liked to play in Maine. Franklin D. Roosevelt spent most of his summers on Campobello, a small island off the coast of Maine.

Skiing is a popular sport in Maine.

Maine at Work

The people of Maine must work to make money. About one third of the state's workers are employed in the **manufacturing industries**.

Because there are so many trees and **forests** in the Pine Tree State, paper and wood products make a lot of money for the people of Maine.

Because of all the visitors to this beautiful state, **tourism** makes a lot of jobs for people in Maine. Along with tourism comes service jobs. Service is cooking and serving food, working in banks, stores, hotels, and restaurants, among others.

Maine makes a lot of leather and leather products. It is one of the biggest makers of leather in the United States.

Maine's **fisheries** are among the most valuable in the United States. Lobster, ocean perch, sea herring, pollack, cod, clams, sea scallops, and shrimp are the most often caught and sold in Maine.

The state of Maine is surrounded by the **Atlantic Ocean**, Canada, and New Hampshire. Because of its beauty, people, and land, the Pine Tree State is a great place to visit, live, work, and play.

Because of all the forests in Maine, lumber is big business.

Fun Facts

• From 3000 to 5000 B.C. the Red Paint **Native Americans** had a summer settlement near Alton, Maine. They could be considered the first people to vacation in Maine!

• The highest point in Maine is Mount Katahdin. It is 5,268 feet (1,606 meters) tall. The lowest point is at the ocean.

• Maine is the 39th biggest state in the United States. Its land takes up 30,995 square miles (80,277 sq km).

Opposite page: Mount Katahdin.

Glossary

Atlantic Ocean: one of a few large seas that surround continents. This one borders the entire east coast of the United States including Maine.
Crops: what farmers grow on their farm to either eat or sell.
Explorers: people that are one of the first to discover and look over land.
Farming: the business of working on a farm.
Fisheries: a place for catching fish.
Forest: a large area of land covered by trees.
Industry: any type of business.
Manufacture: to make things by machine in a factory.
Minerals: things found in the earth, such as rock, diamond, and coal.
Native Americans: the first people who were born in and occupied North America.
Natural Resources: things like water, minerals, or trees that people use from the earth to make other things.
Pasture: land used for animals to graze in.
Peninsula: a long narrow piece of land that reaches out into the water.
Tourism: a business that serves people who are traveling for pleasure, and visiting places of interest.

Internet Sites

Discover Maine
http://www.discovermaine.com
Discover Maine, Maine's Internet Resource. Complete up to date information on Maine news, weather, business, sports, web sites, travel and vacation, computing, and events.

The Maine Internet Index
http://www.mbeacon.com/ndx/ndx1.html
The Maine Index is a continuously growing list of Maine resources, ranging from the simplest individual home site to the most complex commercial and educational sites.

The Maine Resource Guide
http://www.maineguide.com
Maine's Home on the Internet–the Maine Resource Guide! From here, you can access all sorts of vacation, travel and business information about Maine.

These sites are subject to change. Go to your favorite search engine and type in Maine for more sites.

PASS IT ON

Tell Others Something Special About Your State

To educate readers around the country, pass on interesting tips, places to see, history, and little unknown facts about the state you live in. We want to hear from you!

To get posted on ABDO & Daughters website E-mail us at "mystate@abdopub.com"

Index

A

Abnaki 12
Acadia National Park 4, 23, 24
African Americans 18
Androscoggin River 20
Atlantic Ocean 4, 7, 21, 23, 30
Augusta 6, 11, 16, 20, 28

B

Bush, George 16, 19, 21
Bradley, Milton 18

C

Cabot, Sebastian 10, 12
Canada 7, 10, 18, 24
Casco Bay 20

F

farming 8
fishing 20, 21, 24
forests 4, 26
French 10, 14, 18

K

Kennebec River 20

L

Lewiston 20
Longfellow, Henry Wadsworth 6, 18

M

Millay, Edna St. Vincent 6, 18
minerals 8
Mount Katahdin 6, 22, 28

N

Native Americans 10, 14, 18

P

parks 24
pine tree 4, 18, 22, 24, 26, 27

Portland 6, 11, 16, 18, 20, 28

R

river 6

S

settlers 10, 14, 18

T

tourism 26

W

White Mountains 22